THE 1960
WINTER OLYMPICS

THE 1960
WINTER OLYMPICS

David C. Antonucci

ARCADIA
PUBLISHING

Published by Arcadia Publishing
Charleston, South Carolina

Library of Congress Control Number: 2013950225

For all general information, please contact Arcadia Publishing:
Telephone 843-853-2070
Fax 843-853-0044
E-mail sales@arcadiapublishing.com
For customer service and orders:
Toll-Free 1-888-313-2665

Visit us on the Internet at www.arcadiapublishing.com

To Jenny and Dominic, for their enduring love and support

CONTENTS

ACKNOWLEDGMENTS

This book would not be possible without the cooperation of many photographic contributors who generously allowed their work to be enjoyed by many. The author is deeply appreciative for the use of their valuable and unique images.

Bill Briner was an official Olympic photographer whose body of work best represents the essence of the 1960 Winter Olympics. Eddy Starr Ancinas was one of 12 official Olympic guides and writes extensively about travel and ski history. The Auburn Ski Club's Western America SkiSport Museum and its executive director, Bill Clark, have carefully preserved and curated donated collections from the following photographers: John Corbett, a professional photographer in the Truckee area; Richard Hansen, a spectator at the Winter Olympic Games; Russell Stechshulte, an architect responsible for designing and constructing buildings in the Olympic Park; Randy May, a member of the Olympic Ski Patrol; and Floyd Bedbury, an American speed skater who competed in the Winter Games.

Wendall Broomhall, a two-time Olympian, was chief of race for cross-country events, and Martin Hollay was an Olympic worker who helped construct the cross-country courses and biathlon ranges. Dave Newton was a volunteer official at the McKinney Creek cross-country venue. All three provided important photographs and historical information.

The family of Dr. Stan Batiste has collected rare artifacts and memorabilia and put them on public display in Tahoe City. Robert Bonner was a spectator at the Winter Olympic Games. Raleigh DeGeer Amyx is a collector of rare and significant American artifacts. Former professional figure skater Joyce Blackstone provided analysis for descriptive captions for figure skating.

The Walt Disney Family Museum preserves and curates the most extensive collection of Walt Disney artifacts, including objects associated with the 1960 Winter Olympics. The Squaw Valley Ski Museum Foundation seeks to build a permanent ski and Winter Olympics history museum in Squaw Valley.

INTRODUCTION

The 1960 Winter Olympics, known officially as the VIII Olympic Winter Games, began on February 18, 1960, and continued 11 full days through February 28, 1960. Competition events occurred at the California ski resort of Squaw Valley and on the California side of Lake Tahoe, near the vacation community of Tahoma. It was the first complete Winter Games site built from the ground up exclusively for the winter sports competition and in a compact and efficient configuration.

Hailing from 30 countries, 665 athletes competing as amateurs converged to participate in 27 events, including Alpine and Nordic skiing, figure skating, ice hockey, speed skating, biathlon, and ski jumping. Athletes were lodged in a self-contained and restricted-access Olympic Village within walking distance to all competition venues except for Nordic skiing and biathlon.

In Alpine skiing, Germany, Austria, Switzerland, and France dominated the medal counts, but American skier Penny Pitou won two silver medals, and Canadian Anne Heggtveit won a gold medal. Americans Carol Heiss and David Jenkins both received gold medals in individual figure skating. Soviet speed skaters Eugeni Grishin and Lidiya Skoblikova each earned two gold medals in their respective events. German Helmut Recknagel ended Scandinavian domination of the ski jumping with a gold medal and near-perfect jumping scores. The underdog American ice hockey team thunderstruck the Winter Games by going undefeated, overpowering the Soviets, and going on to win the first gold medal in ice hockey for the United States. Finnish cross-country skier Veikko Hakulinen was the most decorated athlete of the games, earning three medals.

The VIII Olympic Winter Games were the watershed for a number of significant Olympic firsts that changed the course of the Olympics. Events were timed electronically, and scoring was tabulated and reported by a computer. Ice events were held on artificially chilled ice. Women were admitted to speed skating competition. Custom-built cross-country courses were prepared using powered mechanical grooming equipment. The sport of the Olympic biathlon debuted here. CBS-TV broadcast live 31 hours of coverage throughout the host country. Elaborate opening, closing, and award ceremonies and extensive Olympic Park decorations were directed by Walt Disney.

This patch shows the symbolic design of the logo for the VIII Olympic Winter Games. Made of yellow, blue, and red triangles arranged over a white background, it symbolized a star-shaped snowflake. The center triangle replicated the roof line of Blyth Memorial Arena with an overlay of the Olympic rings. Text in a circular border defined the official numeration, its location, and the year. (Courtesy of the Batiste Family Collection.)

Medals for first, second, and third place were struck in bronze and then plated in gold or silver or left in bronze. On the front were the profiles of a man and woman, with raised lettering stating the official name of these Winter Games. On the reverse were the Latin words *Citius, Altius, Fortius*, translating to "Faster, Higher, Stronger," with the Olympic rings and the engraved name of the event. (Courtesy of the Raleigh DeGeer Amyx Collection.)

1

EARLY SQUAW VALLEY
SKI HISTORY

For millennia, Squaw Valley was a summer grounds for Washoe Native Americans; later, it was part of a nearby mining boomtown and a remote cattle ranch. Squaw Valley lay largely unnoticed. In 1931, a young man and all-round skier from Reno visited the valley and immediately became consumed by his vision of a grand destination ski resort. Wayne Poulsen acquired a key parcel in 1943 and began soliciting investors to bring his vision to reality after World War II.

Poulsen connected with Alexander Cushing in 1948, and the two agreed to launch a ski area. Poulsen provided the land and management expertise, and Cushing infused capital from his connections on the East Coast. The partnership of the two head-strong and visionary entrepreneurs was short lived. Cushing assumed control just before the ski area's grand opening in November 1949. Poulsen retreated to undertake development of the cattle ranch that he now controlled.

Following the burst of activity surrounding the Olympics in 1960, the mountain resort steadily expanded, adding terrain, lift capacity, gondola (1963), cable car (1969), and on-mountain amenities. The ski area was largely a day-use operation, relying on daily drive-up clientele and the bed base in the nearby historically summer resort towns of Tahoe City, Kings Beach, and Truckee.

Over the course of 25 years, beginning in the 1980s, the ski area gained control of key properties on the mountain and at the head of the valley, including many of the surviving Olympic structures, such as Blyth Memorial Arena. Important additions such as a snow making machine, lodging and commercial properties, children's centers, a funitel (an enclosed ski lift similar to a gondola), and skier lockers appeared during this time. In 2010, private equity firm KSL Partners acquired majority control of the ski area. Barely a year later, KSL merged with neighbor Alpine Meadows Ski Area to create a super-sized ski resort that catapulted into the exclusive group of large destination ski areas in North America.

Today known as Squaw Valley Ski Resort, the skiing behemoth on the Squaw Valley side consists of 3,600 acres of skiable terrain, 30 lifts, 2 on-mountain service and amenity facilities, and an extensive retail, restaurant, and lodging complex at the base.

In this 1942 aerial photograph is a late-winter overview of undeveloped Squaw Valley. The two-mile-long meadow is covered in snow, with Squaw Creek meandering through its middle. The exceptional mountainous ski terrain lies to the west. During this period, the valley was grazing pasture for sheep and cattle with no year-round residents. (Photograph by Keston Ramsey; courtesy of Bill Briner.)

The westerly portion of Squaw Valley, where the ski area and first lodge would eventually rise seven years later, appears in this late winter 1942 aerial photograph. Vividly apparent is the ample snow cover over the expansive skiable terrain and natural bowls that would make it a world-class winter sports destination in less than 20 years. (Photograph by Keston Ramsey; courtesy of Bill Briner.)

Wayne Poulsen, shown here skiing terrain near Mount Rose in the 1930s, first visited Squaw Valley as a teenager and envisioned its potential as an immense ski resort. He acquired 640 acres of land there and eventually cofounded Squaw Valley Ski Area. He and his spouse, Sandy, raised their family in the valley; the two went on to add residential and commercial improvements in the area. (Courtesy of the Poulsen Family Collection.)

Alexander Cushing was a Harvard-trained lawyer and an avid skier who sought a change in his life. After visiting Squaw Valley with Wayne Poulsen in 1946, the two founded Squaw Valley Ski Area. Cushing controlled the ski area from its opening in 1949 until his death at age 92 in 2006. He is well known for initiating and leading the effort to deliver the VIII Olympic Winter Games to California. (Courtesy Western America SkiSport Museum.)

This early-1950s summer view of the ski area shows the rudimentary base facilities present at the time: a dirt parking area, a 50-room lodge, dormitories, and seasonal residences. The massive mountain in the center is KT-22, so named because it once took an early ascent skier 22 kick turns to descend. Squaw Creek is in the center of the photograph, while tributary Shirley Creek emanates from the lower right. (Courtesy of Bill Briner.)

Taken just after a fresh snowfall, this mid-1950s winter scene shows the base of the Squaw One chairlift, billed at the time as the "World's Largest Double Chairlift." The original Cushing family residence is seen on the right side in this image. Along the back ridgeline, Granite Chief (elevation 9,005 feet) is at the far right. (Courtesy of Bill Briner.)

The original 50-room lodge appears in this photograph. When the lodge first opened on November 24, 1949, it still had no running water, but rooms were available for $1 to $6 per night. In 1954, the lodge burned and was rebuilt to look almost exactly the same. Today, it still stands and is known as Olympic House. (Courtesy of Bill Briner.)

Looking down the Squaw One lift alignment, the base and meadow can be seen below. The lift traveled across 8,200 feet of mountainous terrain with a vertical rise of 2,000 feet and handled 600 skiers per hour. Major steelworks companies at the time rejected the project, saying it was impossible to do and that it was too dangerous to hang two people in the air from a steel rope. (Courtesy of Bill Briner.)

The Beer Garden, one of two bars in the lodge, provided an opportunity for live entertainment and après-ski socializing. Squaw Valley became a favorite of Hollywood elite, including Sophia Loren, Bing Crosby, Gene Kelly, and Andy Devine. Even Alexander Cushing would take to the piano and regale his guests. (Courtesy of Bill Briner.)

The original lodge appears in this summer scene showing guests sunning themselves in the crisp mountain air. Though it was never a major summer destination, visitors to the valley could nonetheless ride horseback, hike, or ride the Squaw One chairlift up to the mountain top for a breathtaking view of the Sierra Nevada and Lake Tahoe in the distance. (Courtesy of Bill Briner.)

2

Winning the Olympic Bid and Disney Imagineering

As Alexander Cushing scanned his morning paper in late 1954, he discovered a brief article that told of the Reno, Nevada, bid to secure the 1960 Olympic Winter Games. His interest peaked, Cushing mused that surely a superior Squaw Valley could submit a credible bid and in the process gain wider public attention, even if the gambit ultimately failed. In less than two weeks, he formulated a proposal and made his pitch to decision makers.

At the January 7, 1955, meeting of the Special Sites Committee of the US Olympic Committee, Cushing captured their endorsement. Squaw Valley would now face off against the powerhouses of European skiing in front of the International Olympic Committee. The decision immediately drew criticism from International Olympic Committee president Avery Brundage, who derided Squaw Valley's qualifications and publicly questioned the Special Sites Committee's competence.

In Paris, France, in June 1955, Cushing presented his imaginative proposal and powerful logic that justified the award to Squaw Valley. Under attack by skeptics and the minions of the European skiing industry, Cushing calmly answered all questions with skill and acumen. After three rounds of voting, Squaw Valley emerged as the chosen site for the VIII Olympic Winter Games by a narrow vote of 32-30.

With just four short years in a region with only a six-month annual construction season, the challenge to plan, build, and test Olympic facilities from the ground up was formidable. Early on, the creative force of Walt Disney was incorporated into the planning, with Disney and his talented staff handling all of the pageantry, which included opening and closing ceremonies, site decorations, entertainment, torch and flame cauldron design, and stages for ceremonial functions. It was a logical role for a man so admired by millions and who had created the world's most creative entertainment empire. Disney's planners forever infused the Olympics with the style, comfort, service, and quality that had become a mainstay at Disneyland Resort. Disney's influences led to the most unforgettable and iconic Winter Games in modern history and permanently elevated the public perception of winter sports.

CALIFORNIA
Squaw Valley

UNITED STATES CHOICE FOR THE WINTER OLYMPICS

The cover of Cushing's Olympic bid invoked the skier's dream of deep fresh snow covering challenging terrain bathed in California sunshine. Inside, the proposal pointed out that past Winter Games had occurred six of seven times on the European continent. Arguing that the Olympics "belonged to the world," Cushing suggested it was time to end to this "quasi-monopoly" so that other nations could benefit from a transplant of the Olympic spirit. Cushing proposed a compact and intimate Winter Games because Squaw Valley was a "natural location where athletes and officials can live together in privacy as friendly sportsmen . . . secluded from commercial pressure and public interference." He urged the choice of Squaw Valley as "an accessible location where spectators residing nearby and apart from the Olympic family can observe the contests at reasonable cost in time, effort, and money." Cushing capped his persuasive pitch by citing the area's 450 inches of average yearly snowfall and assuring the International Olympic Committee, "There has never been a year when the requirements of the Winter Games could not be met." (Courtesy of the Wendall Broomhall Collection.).

Taken from the Olympic bid document, Cushing's vision of an economic, compact, and intimate Winter Games site is reflected in this artist's rendering of the proposed Olympic Park. All competition venues would be in Squaw Valley, with the athletes and officials accommodated at an existing destination hotel complex five miles away in Tahoe City, California. (Courtesy of the Wendall Broomhall Collection.)

The reality of the significant competition and housing infrastructure needed to host the Winter Games is apparent in this scale model of final concept for the Olympic venue. Athletes, coaches, and officials would be housed in the valley in a self-contained village within walking distance of most competition venues. (Courtesy of the Western America SkiSport Museum.)

In this image, an illustrator envisions Walt Disney's initial concepts for decorating the Olympic Park. The flag of each participating country serves as a backdrop as spectators approach the competition areas through the Avenue of Athletes. This was an early conceptual drawing; the shape and location of buildings had not been decided yet. The Avenue of Athletes and the Olympic

Village location changed as it became apparent that hosting the Winter Games would require far more extensive facilities than shown here. (Drawing by Walt Disney Productions; courtesy of the Squaw Valley Museum Foundation.)

This illustration of the Avenue of Athletes from a spectator's point of view shows a scene reminiscent of the 1950s-era entrance to Disneyland in Anaheim, California. In this case, the corridor of sculpted Disney cartoon characters is replaced by sculptures of athletes engaged in each of the Olympic competitions. As this concept sketch was developed later in the planning process, the

ENTRANCE FROM PARKING AREA
CORRIDOR OF SNOW SCULPTURE
1960 WINTER OLYMPIC GAMES, SQUAW VALLEY.

buildings in the background (ice arena and spectator center) had taken on their final form. The rows of flags were later moved to serve as the backdrop for the Tribune of Honor. (Drawing by Walt Disney Productions; courtesy of the Squaw Valley Museum Foundation.)

Walt Disney visualized the Tribune of Honor as the focal point and backdrop for the Olympic Park. The design of the Tribune of Honor would embody the symbolism of the Olympic spirit with the flame and cauldron, recognize the participating nations with the Tower of Nations displaying each country's crest, and honor the athletes with the statues of a woman holding skis and a man with an arm raised in the Olympic salute. The Olympic rings, symbolizing the five regions of the

world joined in athletic competition, would overarch all. From this elevated stage surrounded by thousands of spectators, Olympic officials would conduct the medal awards ceremony, bestowing gold, silver, and bronze medals to the top three athletes in each competition. This was the first time in Olympic history that a centralized stage was used for the medal awards. (Drawing by Walt Disney Productions; courtesy of the Squaw Valley Museum Foundation.)

The truck in this photograph advertises Disneyland as the official manufacturer of flags and decorations for VIII Winter Games. However, the involvement of the Disney organization went far beyond these basic services. When the Organizing Committee realized the size and scope of Winter Games, it retained the Disney organization to provide ticketing, parking management, and security. (Courtesy of Bill Briner.)

Willy Schaeffler (left), director of skiing events for the organizing committee, confers with Walt Disney on preparations for the upcoming events. After seeing the success of the Winter Olympics, Disney envisioned a destination ski resort near Sequoia National Park. He collaborated with Schaeffler to plan the resort, but it faced stiff opposition from nascent environmental groups. Disney died before the project could break ground, and plans were permanently shelved. (Courtesy of Bill Briner.)

3

OLYMPIC FACILITIES, VENUES, AND STAFF

Given that Squaw Valley lacked almost all the facilities and infrastructure needed to stage the games, hosting the Winter Games required constructing a fully self-contained Olympic "city," with all the amenities needed to serve a maximum daytime population of 50,000 persons over a two-month period.

The architectural firm of Owings, Skidmore, and Merrill did the master planning in 1955–1956. Planners sited the Olympic Park at the head of the valley at the existing base of the small ski area. Construction began in earnest in 1956. Alpine competition courses were laid out on the flanks of the surrounding mountains and completed by 1958. The jumping hill was ready by 1958. Construction of the ice arena began in 1957; ground-breaking for other buildings began the following year.

The planners had the unprecedented opportunity to conceive a winter sports park and athletes' village in close proximity to each other. Within a short walk to all venues in the valley was the Olympic Village, with a one-story equipment building, a multistory athlete center, and four three-story dormitories offering 600 rooms, including common bathing and dining facilities, that housed 1,200 athletes and support staff.

When the organizing committee staff for Nordic events arrived in Squaw Valley in 1957, they were surprised to see that key terrain approved for cross-country skiing had been taken for residences and widening of the access roadway. They scrambled to relocate the cross-country skiing venue 15 miles south of Squaw Valley to Lake Tahoe, near the seasonal community of Tahoma. Surprisingly, more ski racing events were held there than in the valley.

From an original 1955 estimate of $1 million, the final capital cost of the 1960 Winter Olympics came in at $15 million.

Key to the success of the Winter Games was the involvement of the military and scores of volunteers. The Department of Defense supplied 750 military troops, another 250 civilian personnel, and 200 pieces of military equipment. Volunteers numbered in the thousands, with many coming from the ranks of returning GIs from the 10th Mountain Division. In all, 5,000 people, including athletes, worked to stage the Winter Games.

This winter 1958 image shows the unique roof line of the ice arena under construction. The building featured an exceptionally flexible and economical design. In 1958, it won a prestigious first prize among 600 entries in the Progressive Architecture Design Awards, sponsored by *Progressive Architecture* magazine. Architect Russell Francis Stechshulte oversaw the design and construction of these and other Olympic Park structures. (Courtesy of Bill Briner.)

This summer 1958 view shows Papoose Peak framed by the visible roof beams and joists of the ice arena. The wide spaces between the structural members indicate that the roof was not designed to hold a major snow load. Instead, heat from the production of ice was channeled up to the roof to melt any accumulated snow. (Photograph by Russell Stechshulte; courtesy of Squaw Valley Museum Foundation.)

Construction crews raise the specially fabricated Olympic rings that officially christened the nearly complete ice arena in 1959. This image shows the north end of the arena, which was not enclosed due to International Olympic Committee rules. The bleacher unit in the foreground was designed to swing outward to face the speed skating oval and Tribune of Honor. (Photograph by Russell Stechshulte; courtesy of Squaw Valley Museum Foundation.)

This sign at the entrance to the Olympic Park announced the extensive involvement of the federal government, through the US Forest Service, in constructing and staging the Winter Olympics. Congress appropriated $2.8 million to cover construction of the ice arena, to be administered by the Forest Service. In addition, Tahoe National Forest staff provided avalanche control over the mountain. (Courtesy of Bill Briner.)

This view from the old KT-22 double chairlift shows the extent of facilities occupying the valley during the staging of the Winter Olympics. In the foreground is the Olympic Park, with the ice arena and speed skating oval most prominent. In the background is the parking area, spread out over the meadow. (Courtesy of Bill Briner.)

This aerial overview, taken during the height of the Olympic events, shows the heart of the Olympic Park. Prominent is the ice arena, speed skating oval, and east practice rink. Thousands of spectators gathered around the landing zone for the ski jump and finish area for the women's giant slalom while these competitions were in progress. (Courtesy of Bill Briner.)

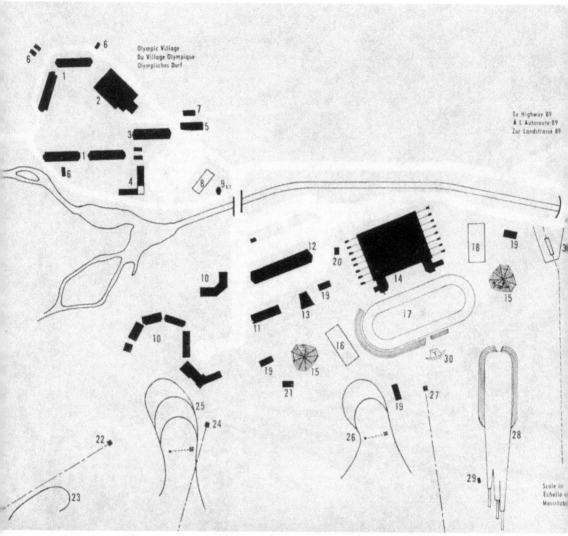

This map, from an athlete's guide to ski events, illustrates the compact and comprehensive layout of the Olympic Park and the Olympic Village. Except for the cross-country and biathlon, all venues were within walking distance of each other, with multiple venues visible simultaneously from various locations around the Olympic grounds. (Courtesy of the Wendall Broomhall Collection.)

Blyth Memorial Arena was named in honor of Charles R. Blyth, the founding chair of the California Olympic Commission, who died in 1959. The arena provided seating for 8,500 spectators and standing room for another 1,500. It was the centerpiece and theme building for the Olympics and hosted the hockey and figure skating events. In 1983, it collapsed under excessive snow load and was demolished. (Courtesy of Bill Briner.)

This is one of two identical spectator centers sponsored by the states of California and Nevada. Each building provided food service, first aid, restrooms, and souvenir sales. Their strategic locations at each end of the Olympic Park and the unique design features that created maximum window space allowed spectators to watch various events simultaneously from inside the buildings. The buildings still remain in use today. (Courtesy of Bill Briner.)

Innsbruck, Austria, the site of the 1964 Olympic Winter Games, hosted this building as a promotional venture to encourage attendance at those games. Innsbruck was heavily favored to win the bid for the 1960 Olympic Winter Games but lost in an upset to Squaw Valley. The structure remains in use, although it has been heavily remodeled. (Courtesy of Bill Briner.)

In the center of this photograph are the six buildings that constituted the Olympic Village, where 1,200 athletes, coaches, and trainers were housed. The village was fully self-contained with a dining common, recreation rooms, lounge, post office, banking center, equipment storage, and physical therapy facilities. The three back buildings are still in use today as timeshare condominiums and corporate offices. (Courtesy of Bill Briner.)

Members of the Unified German team enjoy the bright California sunshine on the deck adjacent to the Olympic Village dining room. Normally closed to the press and public, this was a rare opportunity to have direct access to the athletes while they were inside the Olympic Village. (Courtesy of Bill Briner.)

This overview of the jumping hill, taken during practice, provides a breathtaking look from the athlete's perspective. A ski jumper has just descended the inrun for the 80-meter jump and is airborne over the specially contoured terrain beyond the take-off point. At the time, this was the largest Olympic jumping hill in the world. (Courtesy of Bill Briner.)

Another perspective of the jumping hill looking upward from beyond the landing area shows the two inruns leading to the 80-meter jump (left) and the 60-meter jump, the latter used for the ski jumping part of the Nordic combined competition. The hill was considered exceptionally favorable because of its north orientation away from the sun and the protection from crosswinds by the dense forest. (Courtesy of Bill Briner.)

Forerunner Egon Zimmerman I of Austria prepares to descend the men's giant slalom course on KT-22. A forerunner's job is to make sure all tracks and lines are adequately skied in prior to the race. The course had an average slope of 31 percent and was 5,905 feet long. (Courtesy of Bill Briner.)

A ski racer in a low, aerodynamic drag position, called a tuck, approaches the finish line for the women's giant slalom competition. The finish line came after skiing 4,265 feet on a vertical drop of 1,253 feet, ending on the valley floor near the speed skating oval. (Courtesy of Bill Briner.)

A ski racer speeds toward the finish line of the men's slalom competition after navigating 1,935 feet over a vertical drop 708 feet on the north-facing slope of KT-22. The finish area was on the valley floor near the Squaw Valley Lodge. The existing Exhibition and Searchlight ski trails approximate the original Olympic course. (Courtesy of Bill Briner.)

The finish of the women's slalom was on the valley floor, near the west end of the speed skating oval. As she approached the finish line, a top racer would have skied 1,575 feet down the 38-percent average slope of Papoose Peak in less than two minutes. (Courtesy of Bill Briner.)

THE 1960 WINTER OLYMPICS

The Squaw Valley Chapel was a futuristic design of a sweeping concrete shell floating on glass walls. Built by 11 major Protestant organizations for the Olympics at a cost of $140,000, the 150-seat chapel sits on land donated by the Poulsen family. It still serves a small congregation and hosts community events. (Photograph by David C. Antonucci.)

What appears in this photograph to be an outhouse is actually the surviving remnants of what is known as the "Skier's Chapel" that served Olympic cross-country ski competitors. Tucked away from the main access trail to the McKinney Creek Stadium, it appears to have been constructed by Europeans. Inside was a small altar built of hand-painted ceramic tiles decorated with religious symbols. (Photograph by David C. Antonucci.)

Accommodating the day's influx of automobiles required expansive space and creativity. US Navy Seabees constructed this temporary parking lot for 9,000 vehicles by compacting snow mixed with water and sawdust from local mills. The owner of the site, Wayne Poulsen, refused to allow organizers to pave the environmentally sensitive meadow, forcing them to come up with a less harmful solution. (Courtesy of Bill Briner.)

Spectators enter the ticketing portal between the parking area and the Olympic Park. All-day passes were $7.50 for the valley events of ski jumping, Alpine skiing, and speed skating and $15 for Blyth Arena events. An individual hockey game or figure skating event was $3. (Courtesy of Bill Briner.)

In this view looking east across the Olympic Park just days before the beginning of Olympic events, a number of facilities can be seen already in use. In the foreground is the west ice rink, with skating practice underway, the speed skating oval, and Nevada Olympic Center in the middle distance; in the distance, the temporary parking lot in the meadow can be seen. (Courtesy of Bill Briner.)

Curious spectators peer through the windows of the IBM Data Processing Center that housed the computer used to tabulate and produce competition results for the first time in Olympic history. The unit was provided information through a network of 1 million feet of cable and boasted a storage capacity of 5 megabytes. The building is still in use as a ski rental shop. (Courtesy of Bill Briner.)

Walt Disney's realization of the artistic centerpiece of the Olympic Park was the elevated stage of the Tribune of Honor. It was backed by the 80-foot tall Tower of Nations, displaying the crests of all 30 participating nations and flanked by statues of athletes in the style of snow sculptures. At its center, the flame symbolizing the Olympic spirit burned in its elevated cauldron. (Courtesy of Bill Briner.)

Originally the idea of Walt Disney, sculptures lining the south side of the Avenue of Athletes depicted a biathlete shooting at a target, a hockey goalie, a female Alpine skier, and an airborne ski jumper. State and local government organizations paid $3,000 to sponsor a sculpture. (Courtesy of Western America SkiSport Museum.)

The north side of the Avenue of Athletes featured sculptures of a female speed skater, a male speed skater, a male Alpine skier, and a ski jumper. There were at total of 30 sculptures spread throughout the Olympic Park, 21 men and 9 women, symbolizing the sports of the Winter Olympics. Each freestanding figure was approximately eight feet high and mounted on an eight-foot pedestal. (Courtesy of Bill Briner.)

Here, clockwise from the top left, sculptures depict a male Alpine skier, a female figure skater, a male speed skater, and a ski jumper. Under the supervision of Disney's director of decor John Hench, the sculptures were fabricated of papier-mâché laid over a wire-mesh frame and covered with stucco. (Clockwise from top left, three courtesy of Western America SkiSport Museum and one courtesy of Bill Briner.)

1960 Olympic Ski Patrol

Members of the Olympic Ski Patrol pose with California governor Edmund G. "Pat" Brown (light sweater) and Alexander Cushing (gray blazer). The Olympic Ski Patrol provided a range of services, including rendering of first aid, transport of injured competitors, honor guard for the Olympic torch, avalanche control, and Olympic flag bearers at the opening and closing ceremonies. (Courtesy of Western America SkiSport Museum May Collection.)

A force of 300 US Marines from the Mountain Warfare Training Center and Camp Pendleton and Army soldiers from Fort Lewis were used to groom Alpine ski courses. Here, they are shown marching locked arm-in-arm in a "V" formation as they manually boot-packed an Alpine ski course. Behind them, Marines on skis would side-slip down the course to smooth out the surface. (Courtesy of Bill Briner.)

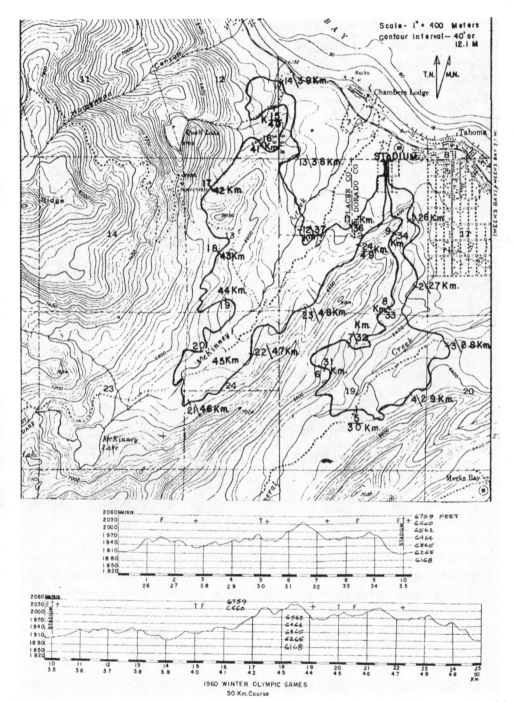

The Organizing Committee submitted this official course map for the 50-kilometer (31-mile) race for certification by the International Ski Federation, the governing body for cross-country ski racing. Racers did two 25-kilometer (15.5-mile) laps, bringing them to the stadium five times, including the start and finish. Checkpoints occurred at one-kilometer (0.62-mile) intervals to verify the skier traversed the entire course. (Courtesy of Western America SkiSport Museum.)

This 1959 aerial photograph shows the location and extent of the McKinney Creek venue for cross-country and biathlon events on the west shore of Lake Tahoe, near Tahoma, California. The site was selected in 1957 as an alternative to Squaw Valley because of the expansive terrain needed for the inaugural biathlon competition and the loss of skiable terrain in Squaw Valley due to speculative land development. (Courtesy of Bill Briner.)

Chief of race Wendall Broomhall (left) and chief of course Allison Merrill were responsible for cross-country events. Together, they designed the first cross-country ski area in the United States and invented the mechanical snow grooming technique that subsequently found widespread use in the ski industry. Broomhall would go on to serve again as chief of race for cross-country events at the 1980 Winter Olympics. (Courtesy of Wendall Broomhall Collection.)

The California Olympic Commission constructed this temporary administrative building at the McKinney Creek Stadium to support race officials, timekeepers, and communications equipment. Press representatives were assigned to the roof deck, where they had a commanding view of action in the stadium. (Courtesy of Bill Briner.)

This aerial view shows the layout of the McKinney Creek Stadium with the finish area and administrative building. The stadium was built in an undeveloped lot and block subdivision with only dirt streets pioneered in. Following the Olympics, the stadium was removed, and land owners proceeded to build vacation homes in the subdivision. (Courtesy of Bill Briner.)

This clock at the McKinney Creek venue showed the local time. Venerable Swiss watchmaker Longines-Wittnauer Watch Company was the official timekeeper for all competitions because of its extensive experience in timing of sporting events. The company generously donated use of all equipment and personnel. (Courtesy of Bill Briner.)

Longines's personnel in the McKinney Creek Stadium office observed and timed cross-country ski competitions. A highly precise quartz timepiece, loosing only one second every 300 years, was at the heart of the custom-built timing system. In the cross-country races, a photocell and relay at the finish line signaled the arrival of a skier for instantaneous printing of the elapsed time. Parallel manual timing occurred but was unneeded. (Courtesy of Bill Briner.)

The temporal nature and thriftiness of the Olympic Commission are evident here in the use of this military-surplus Quonset hut as a waxing and equipment building at the McKinney Creek Stadium. The facility was located on private land, and the owners stipulated complete removal of the improvements after the Olympics; today, the site is occupied by a luxury vacation home. (Courtesy of Bill Briner.)

Much of staffing of the Olympic events was supplied by thousands of volunteers and paid part-time workers. Volunteers worked in many capacities such as ski patrol, interpreters, public information, course marshals, and race assistants. This photograph shows the many volunteers and paid personnel that helped stage the cross-country races. Many of the workers were veterans of the 10th Mountain Division during World War II. (Courtesy of Martin Hollay Collection.)

4

OPENING, AWARDS, AND CLOSING CEREMONIES

Ceremony, symbolism, and pageantry have long been complementary elements to the Olympic movement's themes of athleticism, balance in life, world peace, and equality. With California hosting the Winter Games, it was not surprising that the entertainment aspects of Hollywood would become an integral part of the production. The leadership by Walt Disney as pageantry chair assured that participation. Disney and the Olympics was a perfect match. The creator of the Magic Kingdom was an avid skier and part owner of the Sugar Bowl Ski Area near Donner Summit.

Disney envisioned an exciting and colorful made-for-TV opening gala punctuated by music and thunderous sounds. Opening ceremonies incorporated 3,680 high school students—1,322 musicians and a 2,358-voice choir—in addition to the Marine Corps Band. Thousands of balloons and 2,000 white pigeons acting as stunt doubles for the doves of peace took flight as cannons fired the flags of nations into the air. Speeches, the Olympic oath, and the lighting of the Olympic flame were capped by a spectacular daytime fireworks show.

A fanfare recital performed by a sextet of herald trumpets accompanied by fireworks announced each day's medals awards ceremonies at the Tribune of Honor. The Marine Corps Band played inspiring music as the ceremony started. The honored athletes mounted a three-platform podium, with the gold medal recipient standing in the middle on a raised platform, the silver medal recipient to the gold medalist's right on a lower platform, and the bronze medal recipient to the left on the lowest platform. The national flags of the medalists unfurled on flagpoles in front of each respective medalist. An official Olympic representative presented the medals, followed by the playing of the anthem of the gold medal athlete's country as the thousands of spectators stood in honor of the victorious athletes.

The venerable TV host Art Linkletter served as entertainment director under Disney for the nightly entertainment of athletes in the Olympic Village. Prominent American singing and dancing talent Danny Kaye entertained one night. Another night followed an Old West motif, with a saloon facade and mock gunfight show imported from the Horseshoe Saloon at Disneyland.

Spectators trudge through nearly a foot of freshly fallen snow for the opening ceremonies. However, they need not to hurry—the surprise snowstorm delayed the opening ceremony by one hour to allow Vice Pres. Richard M. Nixon's motorcade to arrive from Reno, Nevada. If it continued, organizers planned to curtail the opening festivities, but director of pageantry Walt Disney would not relent. (Courtesy of Western America SkiSport Museum Hansen Collection.)

Walt Disney's controversial decision was prescient; as the Olympic color guard entered, the skies cleared, and Squaw Valley basked in sunshine as the opening ceremony unfolded. Spectators and high school bands gathered around the Tribune of Honor, where American speed skater and torchbearer Kenneth Henry ignited the cauldron. One hour later, as the ceremonies wound down and the crowd dispersed, the fierce snowstorm resumed. (Courtesy of Bill Briner.)

The creation of an artistic and functional Olympic torch was another Walt Disney–inspired change, brought to life by designer John Hench. His design embodied a smaller version than previous models, making it a more manageable size and weight for torch bearers. During the relay, the top of the shaft had a black grip added for comfort and security. (Photograph by Jim Smith; courtesy of the Walt Disney Family Museum.)

OPENING, AWARDS, AND CLOSING CEREMONIES

With Greece leading the parade of athletes, participating nations marched into Blyth Memorial Arena in alphabetical order. Here, the full complement of Canadian athletes is visible. Snow has blown partly into the arena through its open wall; accumulation was windrowed to provide standing room for the teams. (Courtesy of Dave Newton.)

Each of the 30 participating countries marched into the opening ceremony as a group, accompanied by a salvo of daylight fireworks. Here the Unified German team marches under the banner of the historical German flag with the Olympic rings in place of the respective coat of arms for East and West Germany. (Courtesy of Western America SkiSport Museum Hansen Collection.)

Inside Blyth Memorial Arena, the standing-room-only audience has risen to its feet in honor of the athletes as they enter during the opening ceremonies. The teams for Hungary and Iceland pass the appreciative crowd; the contingents from Australia and Austria are already in place. (Courtesy of Eddy Ancinas.)

The Canadian team marched into the arena, followed by Chile. Canada fielded athletes who participated in 22 of the 26 total competitions. Canadian athletes emerged from these Winter Games with two gold medals and one each of silver and bronze. In the background, the bleacher section has been swung outward toward the speed skating oval and Tribune of Honor. (Courtesy of Eddy Ancinas.)

Teams from various nations stand assembled on the floor of the arena while other nations, including the United States, are still parading along the speed skating oval. The elevated platform on the edge of the arena supported the CBS-TV camera crew that televised the ceremonies live across the United States. The raging snowstorm temporarily caused poor visibility for spectators inside and outside the arena. (Courtesy of Bill Briner.)

The US National Ski Patrol served as the honor guard and flag bearers for the Olympic flags during both the opening and closing (shown here) ceremonies. Eight ski patrol members served as the honor guard for the Olympic torch as it was carried down Little Papoose Peak by Olympic Alpine skiing two-time gold medalist Andrea Mead Lawrence. (Courtesy of Western America SkiSport Museum May Collection.)

At the Tribune of Honor, the US Marine Corps Band under the direction of Lt. Col. Albert Schoepper was the official band for all ceremonies. It played the national anthem of the nation receiving the gold medal during the award ceremony. This is the same band that has provided music for the Office of the President of the United States and has been "the President's Own" since 1801. (Courtesy of Bill Briner.)

Explorer Boy Scouts raised the flags of participating nations on flagpoles designed and placed by the Walt Disney staff. A total of 125 Scouts served as flag raisers, messengers, and crowd control assistants. The aluminum flagpoles were sponsored by various organizations and corporations and fitted with commemorative plaques. They were distributed to their respective sponsors after the Winter Games. (Courtesy of Bill Briner.)

Following the performance of "The Star-Spangled Banner" by the assembled bands, 30,000 balloons were released as the athletes exited by nation to "Parade of the Olympians." Concurrently with the balloon release, cannons fired the flags of the participating nations into the air; the flags then unfurled and drifted down by parachute to signal the conclusion of the opening ceremonies. (Courtesy of Western America SkiSport Museum Hansen Collection.)

As is the custom with Walt Disney–inspired celebrations, there was a spectacular nightly fireworks display over the Tribune of Honor and Tower of Nations. Fireworks displays have been a part of Disney's productions since their first appearance in 1956 above the Cinderella Castle at Disneyland Resort in Anaheim, California. (Courtesy of Bill Briner.)

A sextet of herald trumpets supplied by the C.G. Conn Company of Elkhart, Indiana, played a fanfare that announced the beginning of a medal awards ceremony at the Tribune of Honor. This would mark the first time that all Olympic medal ceremonies would occur in a central public space with public viewing. (Courtesy of Bill Briner.)

Assisted by official hostess Eddy Ancinas, Organizing Committee member Albert E. Sigal prepares to bestow medals for the women's slalom. At the top of the podium is Canadian gold medalist Anne Heggtveit. To her right is American silver medalist Betsy Snite. German Barbara Henneberger received the bronze medal. (Courtesy of Eddy Ancinas.)

A large crowd gathers to witness the awarding of medals for the men's Alpine downhill competition. Frenchman Jean Vuarnet won the gold medal on revolutionary wood-metal-plastic composite skis designed by Squaw Valley ski instructor Emile Allais for French ski manufacturer Rossignol. Hans-Peter Lanig of Germany took the silver medal, and Charles Bozon of France, also on the Rossignol composite skis, captured the bronze. (Courtesy of Bill Briner.)

On February 28, 1960, the VIII Olympic Winter Games concluded. Flag bearers representing the participating nations framed the podium where International Olympic Committee president Avery Brundage would declare the games concluded. The Marine Corps Band played the national anthems of Greece (origin of the Olympic movement), the United States (host nation), and Austria (host nation for the 1964 Winter Olympics). (Courtesy of Bill Briner.)

Led by the Olympic Ski Patrol color guard, athletes entered the closing ceremonies as 20,000 spectators looked on. As is the custom, the athletes were mixed and no longer segregated by nation. The Olympic flame was extinguished, and thousands of balloons were released, marking the end of the most successful and memorable Winter Games ever. (Courtesy of Western America Ski Sport Museum Hansen Collection.)

5

ALPINE SKIING

Alpine skiing competitions divided themselves into three distinct disciplines—downhill, slalom, and giant slalom—with all three events for men and women. The skiers were required to navigate the courses by skiing through gates formed by pairs of poles. Winners were based on the lowest elapsed time.

The slalom course involved skiing through a series of narrow gates in quick-paced, short-radius turns. The giant slalom was another technical skiing event that forced skiers to thread through gates spaced at a greater distance interval and wider than the slalom. The giant slalom was much longer and challenged racers with more frequent though less severe changes in direction than the slalom. The downhill event was primarily a speed contest over obstacles such as bumps, extreme drops, flats, and jumps with difficult snow conditions thrown in for an increased challenge. Placed on the course chiefly for guidance, the gates were much wider than the giant slalom gates and were within sight of each other.

Men's and women's slalom and giant slalom courses and women's downhill were located on the steep north-facing slopes of KT-22 Mountain and Little Papoose Peak. The finish areas were on the valley floor adjacent to the Olympic Park. The men's downhill course started much higher up and farther west on Squaw Peak with a mid-mountain finish. All courses were laid out by University of Denver's ski coach Willy Schaeffler, director of ski events for the Organizing Committee.

The victories in men's Alpine events were dominated by the European countries that claimed territory in the Alps—France, Germany, Austria, and Switzerland. France and Austria alone claimed seven of the nine possible medals. The same was not true for the women's Alpine events. While the formerly listed European countries had a strong showing, more than half the medals were claimed by the United States, Canada, and Italy. American Penny Pitou earned two silver medals, while a silver medal was also won by teammate Betsy Snite.

The start area for the men's downhill Alpine skiing competition was at an elevation of 8,881 feet, just below Squaw Peak, which can be seen in the background. Here, a competitor begins his run, which will plunge him 2,487 feet vertically to the finish line. The racers completed the course in 2 to 2.5 minutes and reached average speeds of 46 to 55 miles per hour. (Courtesy of Bill Briner.)

A competitor in the men's downhill competition skis though gates on the middle section of the course. The staff member in the foreground is an official Olympic course marshal, responsible for observing racers to make sure they complete the course properly. The other staff member is a course maintenance person, who repairs the course after each run to ensure conditions remain constant during racing. (Courtesy of Bill Briner.)

In this view, the finish area of the men's downhill competition course can be seen. After skirting the north flank of Squaw Peak, the course generally followed the canyon of Squaw Creek to the finish area. The finish was located just above and west of the Olympic Park. (Courtesy of Bill Briner.)

German Alpine racer Willy Bogner struggles to retain his balance as he becomes airborne during his run on the men's downhill course. Bogner, a member of the family associated with Bogner sportswear company of Germany, was fifth to start and finished in ninth place with a total elapsed time of 2:09.7. (Courtesy of Bill Briner.)

THE 1960 WINTER OLYMPICS

American Alpine skier Scott Gorsuch approaches the finish area of the men's downhill course. Gorsuch placed 14th overall with an elapsed time of 2:11.0, five seconds behind gold medalist Jean Vuarnet of France. Gorsuch staked the highest placement among the four US skiers who participated in this event. (Courtesy of Bill Briner.)

Enthusiastic spectators cheer on Frenchman Jean Vuarnet during his gold medal–winning run on the men's downhill course. Vuarnet, who would go on to be associated with the eponymous eyewear company, posted a time of 2:06.0 with an average speed of 55 miles per hour. He later publicly "apologized" for breaking California's speed limit law. (Courtesy of Bill Briner.)

These two views of the men's giant slalom course on KT-22 Mountain during training runs show its steepness and difficulty. In the photograph above, the upper part of the course appears with an average slope of 49 percent, which demanded exceptional ski weighting and edging skills to negotiate the gates. The photograph to the right shows the middle part of the course, with its more gentle slope of 25 percent. The gates are spaced farther apart in comparison to the slalom course. The actual competition event was televised live and required the use of two TV cameras stationed along the course. (Both courtesy of Bill Briner.)

American skier Frank Brown attacks the men's slalom course on KT-22 Mountain during the second week of the Winter Games. Brown, an architectural student from McCall, Idaho, was first in the National Alpine Combined Competition in 1958. After a lackluster initial run on the slalom course, he executed the 12th-fastest time on his second attempt among a field of 69 competitors. (Courtesy of Bill Briner.)

Takashi Takeda of Japan clears a gate on the men's giant slalom course. Takeda, a university student, celebrated his 21st birthday the same day as the competition. The runner-up to the 1959 Intercollegiate Alpine Ski Championship in Japan, Takeda placed 44th in a field of 72 slalom racers at the Winter Games. (Courtesy of Bill Briner.)

ALPINE SKIING

Just turned 18, Willy Bogner of the Unified German team inspects the men's slalom course during a pre-race preview session in the photograph to the right. Bogner skis the slalom course in the photograph below, leading the field after the first run. On his second run, he was disqualified after he fell twice. In a hint of what might come, Bogner shot exclusive film footage inside the athlete's village at Squaw Valley and produced a short documentary for German TV. In 1966, Bogner went on to place fourth in the slalom and fifth in the Alpine combined World Cup competitions. After his ski career, he became a filmmaker of skiing movies and served as a cameraman in several James Bond movies that featured skiing scenes. Eventually, he returned to Germany permanently to head the family sportswear manufacturing business. (Both courtesy of Eddy Ancinas.)

Matthias "Hias" Leitner of Austria shows the form on the men's slalom course that won him a place on the awards podium. Leitner was in eighth place after his first run. On his second run, he more than made up the difference by turning in the second fastest time. His combined elapsed time was just 1.4 seconds behind teammate Ernst Hinterseer, giving Austria gold and silver in the event. (Courtesy of Eddy Ancinas.)

Charles Bozon was part of the French team that used the game-changing metal-wood-plastic composite Rossignol skis. At age 28, Bozon was a six-time winner of the French Alpine skiing championship. Here, he shows his seasoned expertise and the advantage of the composite skis to win a bronze medal in the slalom. In 1962, he won a gold medal in slalom in the World Ski Championships. He died in 1964 in an avalanche. (Courtesy of Eddy Ancinas.)

Bruno Alberti of Italy, an electrician by trade, weights his uphill ski as he concentrates on skiing through the slalom gate. Alberti's first run was among the slowest. Like many others, he skied a much faster second run, though it was only sufficient to lift him into 20th place among the field of 69 competitors. (Courtesy of Eddy Ancinas.)

Harvard business school graduate Tommy Corcoran proved to be the best American Alpine skier, with a fourth-place finish in the giant slalom competition and a ninth-place finish in the slalom race, shown here. He was on the 1956 Olympic team that competed at Cortina d'Ampezzo, Italy, and was US national slalom and combined Alpine champion in 1958. (Courtesy of Eddy Ancinas.)

Adolf Mathis, a 21-year-old skier on the Swiss Alpine team, sets his ski edges to clear the gate in the men's slalom event. He placed 15th overall. He continued to ski competitively for Switzerland and finished sixth in the slalom event at the 1964 Winter Olympics in Innsbruck, Austria. (Courtesy of Eddy Ancinas.)

Eysteinn Thordarson, age 25, of Iceland was one of only two competitors from that country to contest the men's slalom. Thordarson was Icelandic champion four times in slalom, three times in giant slalom, and two times in downhill. Against the Northern European powerhouses of Alpine skiing, he mustered a respectable 17th-place finish. (Courtesy of Eddy Ancinas.)

A member of the 1956 Olympic team, Penny Pitou was America's best hope to win a medal in Alpine skiing. She did not disappoint. Pitou became the first American woman to win a medal (silver) in the women's downhill, shown here, followed by a silver medal in the giant slalom. (Courtesy of Bill Briner.)

An unidentified French skier attacks the women's giant slalom course as four Olympic course marshals look on. The competition was won by Yvonne Ruegg of Switzerland by a slim 0.1-second margin over Penny Pitou of the United States. The highest-placed French woman captured seventh. (Courtesy of Bill Briner.)

The finish area for the women's slalom course was on the valley floor, near the speed skating oval and between the Tribune of Honor and the west ice rink. The competition was won by Canadian Anne Heggtveit, followed by Betsy Snite of the United States and Barbara Hennenberger of Germany. Hennenberger died in an avalanche during filming of a ski movie in 1964. (Courtesy of Bill Briner.)

Canadian Alpine skier Anne Heggtveit proudly shows the gold medal she won in the women's slalom. Her award was Canada's first-ever Olympic gold medal won in an Alpine skiing event. She subsequently received much recognition for her accomplishments, including induction into Canada's Sports Hall of Fame. (Courtesy of Library and Archives Canada.)

6

BIATHLON

The biathlon is a test of cross-country skiing ability and marksmanship with rifles. In addition to marksmanship, the target shooting is an analog for measurement of the mental and physical fitness of a competitor. Competitors must have endurance and shooting skills in addition to the ability to physiologically calm breathing and heart rate while target shooting.

The International Olympic Committee formerly recognized biathlon as an Olympic sport in 1957 and retroactively added it to the program of events for the 1960 Winter Games. The event was held on the McKinney Creek cross-country trails at Lake Tahoe and the site became internationally recognized as the birthplace of Olympic biathlon.

In its debut form, the modern winter biathlon, as it was known in 1960, involved 20 kilometers (12.4 miles) of cross-country skiing with shooting at five targets at each of the four firing ranges. Target distances and range locations were, respectively, 200 meters (656 feet) after 6.5 kilometers (4 miles), 250 meters (820 feet) at 9.5 kilometers (5.9 miles), 150 meters (492 feet) at 12.4 kilometers (7.7 miles), and 100 meters (328 feet) at 15 kilometers (9.3 miles). The first three ranges were shot in any position, usually prone, while the final range had to be shot from the off-hand (standing) position. Scoring was based on total elapsed time with a two-minute penalty added for each missed target. Each team had a maximum of four male members who competed as individuals for medals; there was no official recognition for overall team performance.

Some competitors pursued a strategy of skiing as fast as possible while hoping their target misses would be minimal and not degrade their overall score significantly. Other athletes raced conservatively, allotting enough time to shoot with accuracy. It was this latter strategy that proved most effective, with the three medalists possessing the best shooting scores. Sweden's only entrant took the gold medal and became biathlon's first Olympic champion. He was followed by the Finnish for the silver medal and the Soviets for the bronze medal.

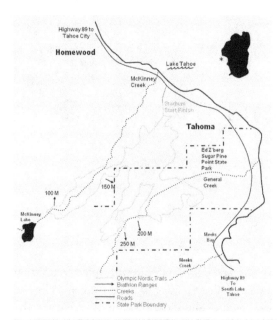

This reconstructed map prepared by researchers shows the route of the 20-kilometer biathlon course and the locations of the four shooting ranges. Two of the four ranges are now protected historical sites within Ed Z'berg Sugar Pine Point State Park. They are accessible by a groomed ski trail in winter and on foot during the hiking season. (Courtesy of the California Department of Parks and Recreation.)

At the McKinney Creek Stadium, Olympic officials prepare to give the start signal to Soviet biathlete Vladimir Melanjin while Jon Istad of Norway waits for his one-minute start interval to elapse. Melanjin had the third-fastest course time, but he missed four targets and eventually placed fourth. (Courtesy of Dave Newton.)

On the 20-kilometer biathlon course, Hungarian Pal Sajgo, an administrative clerk, skis toward the next shooting range. He carried a medium-bore, bolt-action rifle prized for its long range and accuracy. Sajgo's skis are made of lightweight wood laminate materials and have three-pin toe bindings to secure the special boots. (Courtesy of Dave Newton.)

A US biathlete shoots from the prone position at the 200-meter range during the 1959 North American Championships, held on the newly completed Olympic biathlon course. Competitors were required to fire five rounds at five targets at each of four shooting ranges. A two-minute time penalty was added for each missed target. (Courtesy of Bill Briner.)

Official judges observe an American biathlon competitor shoot at the 150-meter firing range during the 1959 North American Championships. American biathletes carried .243-caliber Winchester Model 70 rifles that were preferred for their exceptional accuracy and flat trajectory of the projectile. Workers behind a protective earth backstop changed targets and reported results by wired field phones to score keepers at the McKinney Creek Stadium. (Courtesy of Bill Briner.)

Gold medalist Klas Lestander, a Swedish carpenter, shoots his way into Olympic history at the 150-meter range. Lestander carried a specially modified bolt-action rifle with a folding stock that saved weight. Lestander's race strategy was to ski efficiently and shoot very accurately. Although his overall course time was just average, his perfect shooting score prevented the time penalties that demoted others with faster course times. (Courtesy of Wikimedia Commons.)

7

CROSS-COUNTRY SKIING

Cross-country skiing has a long and rich history that dates back some 4,500 years in the countries of Northern Europe, where travel on skis was a way of life during the winter season. Cross-country skiing was on the program of events for all Olympic Winter Games.

In 1960, cross-country skis were made of laminated woods, usually spruce, hickory, ash, and beech, with a highly curved tip and very narrow width. The skis had camber, or vertical curvature, along the length of the ski and flexed in response to the skier's weight. As the skier placed full weight on one ski, it flattened and special grip wax applied to the center portion of the ski grasped the snow surface, allowing the skier to lunge forward for propulsion. With skis equally weighted, they glided on tips and tails.

Men skied in four different events denoted by their metric distances: 15 kilometers, 30 kilometers, 50 kilometers, and a four-man relay of 10 kilometers each. Women, who were still relatively new to the Olympic sport, raced a shorter distance of 10 kilometers and participated in a three-woman relay of 5 kilometers each. A third type of competition for men only called Nordic combined united cross-country skiing with ski jumping.

The Scandinavian countries of Sweden, Norway, and Finland collectively earned an unbroken and exclusive presence on the winner's podium in Olympic cross-country skiing competition up to the 1956 Winter Games. At that time, the Soviet program of developing winter athletes flexed its muscles with two gold medals and seven lesser medals. The period of 1952–1964 was known as the Jernberg-Hakulinen Era for the two dominant figures in Olympic cross-country skiing. Swede Sixten Jernberg and Finn Viekko Hakulinen accounted for 16 Olympic medals over that time, including five medals at the 1960 Winter Olympics.

The Scandinavian men repelled the Soviets in 1960 by dominating the first two places in all events and forcing them to scramble for two bronze medals out of 12 possible medals. However, the Soviet women continued their dominance by taking two-thirds of the medals in their events.

Andrew Miller of the US cross-country team skis the men's 30-kilometer (18.6-mile) race on the McKinney Creek course. He was the national champion in 1955. Miller placed 38th in the 30-kilometer race at the 1956 Winter Olympics in Cortina d'Ampezzo and raised his placement four years later to 27th. (Courtesy of Dave Newton.)

Andrew Miller enters the finish area in the 30-kilometer (18.6-mile) race. Just over a week later, he skied to a 17th-place finish in the 50-kilometer (31-mile) race. His placement set a high-water mark for American cross-country skiers in Olympic competition, and the record stood until 1976, when Bill Koch earned a silver medal in the 30-kilometer (18.6-mile) race. (Courtesy of Dave Newton.)

CROSS-COUNTRY SKIING

In the 30-kilometer (18.6-mile) race, Norway was represented by four skiers, including Sverre Stensheim, shown here. Stensheim finished 20th, clocking an elapsed time of just under two hours. He later skied to a 10th-place finish in the 50-kilometer (31-mile) and competed again in both events at the 1964 Winter Olympics in Innsbruck, Austria. (Courtesy of Dave Newton.)

Considered old for a cross-country skier at age 30, Swede Lennart Larsson shows the excellent diagonal stride form that carried him to a fifth-place finish in the 30-kilometer (18.6-mile) competition. Larsson had previously won a bronze medal in the 4x10-kilometer (6.2-mile) relay at the 1956 Winter Olympics at Cortina d'Ampezzo, Italy. (Courtesy of Dave Newton.)

THE 1960 WINTER OLYMPICS

Known as the "King of Skis" in 1960, Sixten Jernberg of Sweden won the gold medal in the 30-kilometer (18.6-mile) race. Despite his later starting slot, when the course conditions were slower, Jernberg's elapsed time was 13 seconds better than his next closest rival, teammate Rolf Ramgard. (Courtesy of Dave Newton.)

Also known as the "Gray Ghost," Swede Sixten Jernberg, in his second of what would be three Winter Olympics, skis to gold in the 30-kilometer (18.6-mile) race. Over his 12-year Olympic career, Jernberg won four gold medals, three silver medals, and two bronze medals. In 12 races in Winter Olympics competitions, Jernberg never finished lower than fifth place. (Courtesy of Dave Newton.)

CROSS-COUNTRY SKIING

This overview of the finish line for the men's 15-kilometer (9.3-mile) special race shows the technological advancements in timing. Twin infrared photocell emitters cast invisible beams to the receiver relays. When a skier crossed the line, the beams were broken and a signal sent to the electronic timing device. This marked the first time in Olympic history that electronic timing was used over the traditional hand methods. (Courtesy of Bill Briner.)

A Finnish cross-country skier begins the men's 15-kilometer special race by passing through the photocell beam to start the timing clock. The field of 54 skiers started at intervals of 30 seconds. The course was one loop that required a challenging 1,575 feet of climbing at elevations as high as 6,710 feet. (Courtesy of Bill Briner.)

A small crowd of trailside spectators cheers on cross-country ski racer Lars Olsson of Sweden as he ascends the dividing ridge on the men's 4x10-kilometer (6.2-mile) relay course. Olsson was the lead-off racer for the Swedish team and was first among all first-leg racers to complete his 10-kilometer lap in an elapsed time of 34:56.0. (Courtesy of Dave Newton.)

Norwegian Einar Ostby (bib no. 1) nears the finish line of the third leg of the men's 4x10-kilometer relay. Ostby, who had placed fifth in the 15-kilometer special race, turned in a very fast lap that extended Norway's lead over Finland by a nearly insurmountable 20 seconds. The race would be decided in the fourth leg of the relay. (Courtesy of Dave Newton.)

After nearly 40 kilometers of racing, the men's 4x10-kilometer relay was decided in the final 100 yards. After trailing Norwegian Hakon Brusveen (left) over much of the anchor leg of the relay course, Finnish superstar Veikko Hakulinen surges toward the finish line with a furious double pole stride. (Courtesy of Dave Newton.)

In a superhuman effort over the last few yards, Finn Veikko Hakulinen passes Norwegian Hakon Brusveen and accelerates to the finish line with one final powerful push on both of his poles. Hakulinen erased the Finnish team's 20-second deficit during the end of the fourth leg and crossed the finish line 1.2 seconds ahead of Brusveen. (Courtesy of Bill Briner.)

In a strong but futile effort, Norwegian Hakon Brusveen lunges toward the finish line to claim second place in the men's 4x10-kilometer relay. Just ahead of him is Veikko Hakulinen of Finland, who saved the race for his Finnish team. In appreciation, the Finnish team paraded Hakulinen around the stadium on their shoulders to an approving crowd of 3,000 spectators. (Courtesy of Bill Briner.)

On the course for the 50-kilometer (31-mile) race, Veikko Hakulinen of Finland shows the strength that would carry him to a silver medal. Hakulinen would emerge from the 1960 Winter Games as the most decorated athlete with three medals—gold, silver, and bronze. He finished his career of four Winter Olympics with seven medals in cross-country skiing. (Courtesy of Dave Newton.)

CROSS-COUNTRY SKIING

The scoreboard at the McKinney Creek stadium forecasts what will be the final results of the 50-kilometer race, even though the competition is still underway. In first place is Kalevi Hamalainen (No. 1) of Finland, with a time of 2:59:06. He is trailed by superstar teammate Veikko Hakulinen (No. 26), and Swede Rolf Ramgard (No. 16). Noteworthy on the board is the posted time for American Leo Massa (No. 5). (Courtesy of Dave Newton.)

The Swedish women's cross-country team poses for a group photograph on the dividing ridge of the McKinney Creek racecourse. Three members of the team won gold in the women's 3x5-kilometer (3.1-mile) relay race. The win was protested by the Soviets but was decided in favor of the Swedes after course officials used a spectator's 8-millimeter film to view the alleged infraction. (Courtesy of Dave Newton.)

This iconic portrait of the youthful US Nordic and combined ski team includes a prank on the scoreboard showing the United States finishing first and second in a mythical 10-kilometer race. Members of the team included Joe Pete Wilson, who would go on to create the first private cross-country ski area in the United States, and Peter Lahdenpera, who would serve on the International Biathlon Union. (Courtesy of Bill Briner.)

West German Sportsman of the Year (1960) Georg Thoma poses with 1960 Winter Olympics gold medalists Heidi Schmidt (left) and Ingrid Kramer. Thoma became the first non-Scandinavian in Olympic history to win a gold medal in the Nordic combined when he won at the 1960 Winter Olympics. The Nordic combined competition united ski jumping on the 60-meter (196.9-foot) hill with 15 kilometers (9.3 miles) of cross-country ski racing. (Courtesy Bundearchiv.)

8

FIGURE SKATING

Figure skating derives its name from the tradition of inscribing "school figures" on ice using skates. For many years, executing these figures was a compulsory part of figure skating competition, along with a free or artistic skating performance. Figure skating in its earliest form first appeared in the 1908 Summer Olympics. It has been a permanent part of the Olympics since the first Winter Games in 1924. Both men and women have participated as individuals and in mixed pairs.

For the singles' competition, a majority ranking by a panel of nine judges determined scoring for the compulsory figures and the free skating program on a scale of 0–6 points. Using their scores, the judges ranked the competitors, with the winner receiving the highest composite ranking among all judges. The judges used a complex system of voting that assigned ranks or ordinals to each competitor.

A pair skating team is made up of one man and one woman. In pairs skating, the team functions as one, performing all the moves in a singles' competition, plus additional elements such as lifts, throw jumps, and pair spins. Scoring was done by seven judges using the 6.0 system, with rankings based on a free skating program only.

The four-day competition in Blyth Arena included 26 women from 13 countries. American Carol Heiss, four-time world champion and Olympic silver medalist in 1956, won the gold medal. American Barbara Roles took a bronze medal. American medical student David Jenkins was a three-time world champion, a 1956 bronze medalist, and won gold in the men's singles among a field of 19. Jenkins's gold medal was the fourth straight gold medal for the United States in Olympic competition. In pairs, Barbara Wagner and Robert Paul of Canada won gold, with the American team of Nancy and Ronald Ludington taking bronze.

Karol Divin of Czechoslovakia executes a spectacular jump during the free skating program of the men's figure skating competition. The 24-year-old Divin was a two-time European and eight-time Czechoslovakian champion and highly favored to win gold. He held the lead after completion of the compulsory figures and earned the silver medal. (Courtesy of Eddy Ancinas.)

Medical student David Jenkins of the United States shows his supple and fluid style during the free skating program of the men's figure skating competition. Jenkins executed crossovers, jumps, an open Axel, triple Salchow, triple loop, camel spin, and a flying camel jump-sit. The highly impressed judges awarded him excellent scores, including the only perfect 6.0 in the competition, resulting in a gold medal. (Courtesy of Western America SkiSport Museum Hansen Collection.)

In this iconic image, Sjoukje Dijkstra, an 18-year-old student from the Netherlands, completes her free skating program before an appreciative crowd. Dijkstra was the women's European champion in 1960 and was considered a strong contender for the gold medal. In second place after completion of the compulsory figures, she was awarded the silver medal after her free skating program. (Courtesy of Bill Briner.)

An unidentified male skater executes a balancing move during the men's free skating program. In the background is the unenclosed end of Blyth Memorial Arena, with the moveable bleacher sections turned inward. Hanging down through the open gable is a curtain made of 1.5-inch-diameter braided nylon rope in a partially effective attempt to prevent sunlight from affecting the ice surface. (Photograph by Robert Bonner; courtesy of Edward N. Bonner.)

Judges stand on the ice, prepared to inspect a competitor's compulsory (school) figures. It consisted of 60 percent of the total score for each competitor. The requirement was to skate the original required figure on the ice and repeat three times within a quarter of an inch of the original mark. A skater who was very disciplined in school figures could win the competition over a great performer. (Courtesy of Dave Newton.)

American figure skater Carol Heiss stands at the top of the winner's podium as the Marine Corps Band plays "The Star-Spangled Banner." International Olympic Committee president Avery Brundage (left) presented Heiss with the gold medal in women's figure skating. To Heiss's right is silver medalist Sjoukje Dijkstra of the Netherlands, and to Heiss's left is bronze medalist Barbara Roles of the United States. (Courtesy of Bill Briner.)

FIGURE SKATING

In this photograph, captured during a practice session in Blyth Memorial Arena, a male coach is working with a female singles' competitor in a practice session. Her right leg is on a back outside edge, indicating that she may have just landed a jump. The pair appears to be part of a European team. (Courtesy of Western America SkiSport Museum Hansen Collection.)

During the pair skating competition, this woman is doing a very traditional, if not dated, forward spiral. Her partner rotated her in a circle around him with his right toe pick in the ice and the left foot (skate) on the outside back edge. The modern version of this move is the death spiral. (Courtesy of Western America SkiSport Museum Hansen Collection.)

United German team pair figure skater Marika Kilius poses for a publicity photograph outside the Olympic Village. Kilius and her skating partner, Hans-Jürgen Bäumler, won the silver medal in the pair figure skating. Kilius went on to skate professionally and launch a singing career after winning another silver medal in the pair skating competition at the 1964 Winter Olympics. (Courtesy of Bill Briner.)

In this outdoor session on the West Rink, two female skaters engage in practice. The woman in front is preparing herself for a jump, while the woman in the background is practicing a dance (toe-pick) step. In the background is Blyth Memorial Arena, showing how its roof structure was cable-stayed from the exterior to provide a column-free clear span for the ice sheet. (Courtesy of Bill Briner.)

9

ICE HOCKEY

Ice hockey is a game of speed and fast-paced, nonstop action. Two teams of six players competed on an 85-foot-wide by 200-foot-long ice rink. Players were required to have superb ice-skating agility, tactical aggressiveness, and excellent hand-eye coordination for shooting skill. Games consisted of three 20-minute periods, with timeouts. Infractions resulted in referees sending the offending player to a penalty box to sit out the time penalty.

Olympic officials organized the hockey games into a round-robin tournament. Nine countries fielded teams, totaling 152 men, and competed in 30 games held in Blyth Arena and outdoors on the East Rink. What followed were epic battles on ice, some that metaphorically represented the Cold War rivalry that engulfed the world in 1960.

Canada was the undisputed powerhouse of Olympic ice hockey, with a record of six gold medals, one silver, and one bronze in the last eight Winter Games. The Canadians were favored again, but the upstart 1956 Winter Games gold medalists, the Soviets, were strong contenders also. The United States, despite winning five silver medals and one bronze in seven Olympic attempts, did not seem to have much of a chance of being competitive. In what many considered an over-the-top boast, coach Jack Riley told *Sports Illustrated* that he expected the team would be in the top three at the end of Olympic competition.

The United States went undefeated and captured its first-ever gold medal in Olympic hockey. Czechoslovakia took the silver medal, and the Soviets received the bronze medal. The historic accomplishment by the United States received scant notice at the time. It has since become known as the "Forgotten Miracle" in deference to the legendary "Miracle on Ice" associated with the US Olympic hockey team gold medal at the 1980 Olympic Winter Games.

In a pre-Olympics exhibition match, the United States plays Japan on the outdoor East Rink on February 16. In the foreground are United States team members Robert McVey (No. 8) and Robert Owen (No. 5). The game was a blowout for the United States with 10-0 win over Japan. (Courtesy of Bill Briner.)

In a final-round game against Sweden, Paul Johnson (No. 15) of the United States drives the puck toward the goal as Eugene Grazia (No. 11) readies himself to defend. In the first period, the highly motivated US team jumped to a 4-0 lead. Sweden mounted a comeback in the second period, but it fell short. (Courtesy of Bill Briner.)

A Swedish player moves the puck with US players Rodney Paavola (left) and Roger Christian in pursuit during a final-round game. Christian scored three goals during the game, making him the top scorer on the team. The United States won decisively with a final score of 6-3. (Courtesy of Bill Briner.)

With just 17 seconds left to play in the championship round and leading by one goal, US players Robert McVey (No. 8) and Rodney Paavola (No. 9) put pressure on the Soviets. Immediately thereafter, the Soviet coach made a desperate tactical decision. He pulled his goalie and sent him to the opposing side in a futile attempt to overwhelm the Americans and tie the game. (Courtesy of Bill Briner.)

Overcoming a scoring deficit, the United States inflicted a six-goal scoring rampage on the Czech Socialist Republic (CSR) during the third period of the gold-medal game. Defending the US goal are players Weldon Olson (No. 16), John Kirrane (No. 3), John McCartan (No. 2), and Paul Johnson (No. 15). (Courtesy of Bill Briner.)

The US Olympic hockey team posed for a team portrait during its 1960 Training Tour. Just days before the onset of Olympic play, two players were replaced. The team captain pasted head shots of the replacements over the discharged team members in the first row, third from left, and second row, second from left. (Courtesy of the Squaw Valley Museum Foundation.)

10

SKI JUMPING

The special jumping competition occurred on the 80-meter (262.5-foot) hill on the north flank of Little Papoose Peak. The field was composed of 45 men from 15 countries. This was the final event of the VIII Olympic Winter Games and was conducted in the morning, just before the afternoon's closing ceremonies.

Points awarded by judges for distance and style (form) determined the scoring in ski jumping competitions. Five judges evaluated the competitors' form on a 20-point scale according to preset scoring criteria, with the highest and lowest scores disregarded. The distance was converted to points, and the two scores added to reach a combined total for each jump. Each competitor jumped twice, and his combined scores from both jumps determined his final ranking.

As each jumper shot down the inrun to the takeoff point, he reached a speed of about 55 miles per hour. He stayed aloft about 3.5 seconds before touching down in a Telemark-style stance of skis together with one leg forward, knees bent, and arms outstretched to the sides for balance.

Historically, Olympic jumping competition is a Scandinavian-dominated sport, with Norway holding six gold medals and Finland one gold medal at the start of the 1960 Olympics. At the 1959 North American Championships, Juhani Kärkinen of Finland set the pre-Olympics hill record with a jump of 290 feet.

Helmut Recknagel of the Unified German team broke the Scandinavians' 36-year grip on gold in Olympic jumping competition by holding the lead after both rounds. His long jumping distances of 306 and 277 feet along with his high marks for style set him well ahead of the rest of the field. He was followed by Finland with the silver medal and Austria with the bronze medal.

In this view looking upward toward the starting gate, a US ski jumping athlete slides on long, wide jumping skis down the inrun (ramp) of the 80-meter (262-foot) jumping hill. At the end of the inrun is the take-off point, just above the Olympic rings in this photograph, where the jumper becomes airborne. (Courtesy of Bill Briner.)

SKI JUMPING

These two views of American ski jumpers during practice sessions give differing perspectives of a typical jump. In the photograph to the right, the competitor is in the classic Daescher form, with body bent at the hips, an exaggerated forward lean, and arms held back and tight to the sides for an efficient aerodynamic profile. The photograph below illustrates the vertical trajectory of a typical jump as it follows the contour of the jumping hill, keeping the jumper a safe distance above the snow surface. This competitor is attempting to land on the critical point on the jump hill where he would get a maximum score. (Both courtesy of Bill Briner.)

During a pre-competition practice session, a ski jumper on the 80-meter jump is airborne in this view from the top of the inrun. Below is the landing area and run-out zone on the valley floor. The peaked building in the background is the Nevada Olympic Center for spectators. (Courtesy of Dave Newton.)

The revolutionary form used by Helmut Recknagel of the Unified German team is apparent here. Recknagel is leaned far forward with arms extended ahead in what was dubbed the "Superman technique." This aerodynamic form gave Recknagel additional lift that carried him to the two longest jumps of the competition. This, coupled with his excellent scores for style, enabled him to win the gold medal in the special jumping competition. (Courtesy of Dave Newton.)

The US ski jumping squad poses for a group photograph in front of the ski jumping hill. The highest-placed American was Ansten Samuelstuen, a Norwegian-born Coloradoan, who secured seventh place, ahead of the reigning world champion Juhani Kärkinen of Finland. Other Americans placed 28th, 32nd and 42nd among the field of 45 athletes. (Courtesy of Bill Briner.)

11

S P E E D   S K A T I N G

Speed skating is among the fastest of the human-powered endurance sports where mechanical assist and the influence of gravity do not play a role. Skaters typically reached peak speeds of 37 miles per hour. Competitors raced European-style in heats of two skaters traveling counterclockwise on the 400-meter (1,312.3-foot) oval-shaped ice sheet. The races are time-trial events in which each competitor skates against the clock, with the winner being determined by the overall lowest individual elapsed time among all heats.

For well-conditioned athletes, three external factors—air resistance, ice quality, and altitude—affect speed skating. The speed of a skater is determined 70 percent by air resistance and 30 percent by friction between the skate blade and the ice surface. Altitude played a two-part role. The lower density air reduced air resistance, but the lower percentage of oxygen at the higher altitude of 6,200 feet affected a skater's cardiovascular effectiveness. In addition, the Olympic speed skating oval was artificially refrigerated for the first time in Olympic history. This created a colder, harder, and therefore faster ice surface when compared to the natural ice used in all previous Winter Games.

While sports pundits focused on the artificial ice and altitude as wild cards, public interest focused on the women who were admitted into Olympic speed skating competition for the first time. Because of their rigorous and advanced training techniques, the Soviets and the Soviet Bloc countries fielded especially strong women's teams rivaled only by the Scandinavians.

The Soviet women clearly put their stamp of authority on world speed skating. They earned the gold in three of four races and placed in half of all medal award categories. Only Germany and Poland came close, with two medal winners each, followed by the United States and Finland, claiming one medal each.

Much like the Soviet women, the Soviet men dominated the speed skating competition with two gold medals and one-third of the overall medal awards in speed skating. With six gold medals and 12 medals in total, the dominance of the Soviet speed skating dynasty was an incontrovertible fact in 1960.

Speed skaters warm up on the 400-meter (1,312.3-foot) skating oval while spectators observe the action. This was the first Olympic speed skating oval formed with artificially chilled ice. To the far left are the Tribune of Honor and the Tower of Nations. In the background is the California Olympic Center. (Courtesy of Bill Briner.)

From left to right are speed skaters Floyd Bedbury of the United States, Keith Meyer of the United States, Kjell Backman of Sweden, and Sexten Albinsson of Sweden, who are all warming up before a race on the speed skating oval. Backman won the bronze medal in the men's 1,000-meter (3,280.8-foot) race. (Courtesy of Bill Briner.)

Just after the firing of the starter's gun, Renato de Riva of Italy (No. 27) faced off against Canadian Ralf Olin in a head-to-head speed skating race. Olin raced over four Winter Olympics, achieving his highest placement at 15th in the 10,000-meter (32,808.4-foot) race in the 1964 Winter Games. (Courtesy Western America SkiSport Museum Hansen Collection.)

Floyd Bedbury (right) of the United States closes the gap against a Japanese competitor. The American has extended his right arm to counter balance his inward lean as he rounds the curve. Bedbury set the United States records in speed skating on three different distances and held five Minnesota state titles in road cycling. (Courtesy Western America SkiSport Museum Bedbury Collection.)

American speed skater Jeanne Omelenchuk warms up as she prepares for her race. Omelenchuk was a bicycle racer who added speed skating to her repertoire in the 1950s. At these Olympics, she competed in three speed skating events, achieving 15th place in both the 1,000-meter (3,280.8-foot) and 1,500-meter (4,921.3-foot) women's events. (Courtesy Western America SkiSport Museum Bedbury Collection.)

In a rare tie in the men's 1,500-meter (4,921.3-foot) speed skating race, Roald Aas of Norway and Eugeni Grishin of the Soviet Union (both on top of the podium) receive gold medals from an Olympic official, assisted by Olympic hostess Eddy Ancinas. Boris Stenin of the Soviet Union (right) received the bronze medal in the same event. Grishin also won a gold medal in the men's 500-meter (1,640.4-foot) speed skating race. (Courtesy of Eddy Ancinas.)

SPEED SKATING

12

SPECTATOR EXPERIENCE

This was, perhaps, the first Winter Games to emphasize the importance of spectators, largely due to the influences of Walt Disney. Speaking of the visiting athletes and spectators, Disney declared early on that, "Nothing is more important than creating lasting goodwill among our visitors, and we shall do everything we can to make their stay a happy one." The California and Nevada Olympic Centers specifically accommodated the needs of guests, including food service, warming areas, first aid, viewing balconies, souvenir sales, and restrooms.

The Organizing Committee established a lodging certification program to ensure that providers met standards for reasonable cost, comfort, and safety. Spectators found accommodations nearby at Lake Tahoe and Truckee and as far away as Reno and Sacramento. The California Department of Highways accelerated construction of portions of Interstate 80 to Truckee to handle the daily volume and widened the highway from Truckee to Squaw Valley to four lanes. The availability of onsite parking for 9,000 cars was a grand gesture to California's dependence on the automobile and capped by radio bulletins on traffic conditions.

The Organizing Committee sold a 122-page souvenir program for $1 that contained extensive information about the Olympic sports, local history, competition schedules, and guidance for viewing and enjoying the events. On a daily basis, the committee printed onsite an updated program of schedules and news of the day's events. A wide range of Organizing Committee-licensed souvenirs and memorabilia was available for purchase at Squaw Valley and throughout the region.

Over 1,100 ticket outlets provided readily accessible service to potential spectators. A daily admission ticket to valley events was $7.50 and allowed access to all events viewable outdoors and within the Olympic Park. Seats in the arena for individual events were $3 to $5.

Crowds were immense, especially on weekends and during opening and closing ceremonies. Daily attendance varied from a low of 15,000 to a high of 46,000 on the Sunday following the opening of the Winter Games. Over the course of 11 days of official events, nearly 250,000 people visited the valley and experienced the magic of the Olympic spirit.

CBS-TV paid $50,000 for exclusive broadcasting rights for the 1960 Winter Olympics. Anchored by Walter Cronkite, the network broadcast 31 hours of live coverage nationwide. Broadcasts included the opening and closing ceremonies, full coverage of certain skating, hockey, skiing, and ski jumping events in the valley, and daily highlights. This marked the first time that live television coverage of the Olympics was broadcasted over the airwaves throughout the host country. (Courtesy of Bill Briner.)

In the crowd of spectators, one might see up-and-coming ski filmmaker Warren Miller (center). By 1960, Miller had already made 11 ski films; he went on to direct 38 feature-length ski films by 1987. Miller filmed many extreme skiers coursing the slopes and chutes of Squaw Valley and contributed to its reputation as one of America's finest ski areas. (Courtesy of Bill Briner.)

The 1960 Winter Olympics was a place to show off eccentric skiing-themed outfits, as this gentleman aptly demonstrates. In an era of the legend of Davy Crockett, made popular by Walt Disney, many articles of clothing featured real animal skins and fur as a practical means to ward off winter cold and dampness. (Courtesy of Bill Briner.)

Total attendance over the 11-day Olympic Winter Games was nearly 250,000, with a peak day crowd of 46,100. In the photograph above, the crowd watches the finish of the men's slalom on KT-22 Mountain on a day when 19,000-plus spectators attended the events. In the photograph below, spectators gather on the valley floor to watch the action unfold on the speed skating oval as others take advantage of the gentle slope of the Nevada Olympic Center roof to get a better view. (Both courtesy of Bill Briner.)

Visitor information literature was plentiful and readily available. Clockwise from upper left are a California State Automobile Association Squaw Valley and vicinity map, a Town of Truckee promotional brochure, a pocket guide to events, an official program, an individual ticket to valley outdoor events, a guide to area housing and lodging, and a daily updated schedule of athletic events, ceremonies, and services. (Courtesy of the Batiste Family Collection.)

Many spectators acquired Olympic-themed keepsakes in the form of tableware and decorating items. Key to the sentimental value of these items was the display of the VIII Olympic Winter Games star logo or the Olympic rings on the item. Clockwise from the upper left are a decorative plate, an ashtray, a souvenir spoon, a commemorative platter, and an earthenware beer stein. (Courtesy of the Batiste Family Collection.)

Personal accessories were available for purchase or as giveaway promotional items. Clockwise from the upper left are a woman's scarf illustrating the various competitive Olympic sports, a man's handkerchief with authorized VIII Olympic Winter Games star logo, a Tyrolean-style felt hat, a baseball-style cap with the logo, plastic field glasses with a logo medallion, and a travel bag. (Courtesy of the Batiste Family Collection.)

Embroidered cloth patches were popular collector's items and were often affixed to one's ski parka or sash to signify attendance at the Olympics. Clockwise from the upper left are a VIII Olympic Winter Games star logo, Squaw Valley Ski Area logo, and Blyth Arena patch; an Olympic rings and torch patch; a Harvey's Wagon Wheel Casino commemorative patch; a Squaw Valley Ski Area logo and Blyth Arena with open bleacher sections patch; a chairlift, skier, Blyth Arena, and Olympic rings patch; and an Olympic torch and rings patch. (Courtesy of the Batiste Family Collection.)

These felt pennants are commemorative flags with official and authorized logos and insignia that could be displayed as proof that one attended the VIII Olympic Winter Games. From top, they are a souvenir pennant showing Blyth Arena and the speed skating oval as part of the VIII Winter Olympics of 1960; a pennant emphasizing Squaw Valley as the location of the Winter Olympics; and a pennant incorporating the VIII Olympic Winter Games title with the formal star logo and the Olympic rings. (Courtesy of the Batiste Family Collection.)

Ski pins are highly collectible items that are worn on ski apparel to show one's broad experience at many different ski areas and attendance at prestigious ski competition events. Pin trading among collectors and participants is a very common activity at winter sports events. Clockwise from the top left are a Soviet participation pin; a commemorative Norwegian pin showing the medal tally for Norway—three gold, three silver, and zero bronze medals; an authorized Olympic ski patrol pin; a Winter Olympic attendance pin; a Reno, Nevada, promotional pin; a Squaw Valley Ski Area pin; and an official VIII Olympic Winter Games star logo pin with rings. (Courtesy of the Batiste Family Collection.)

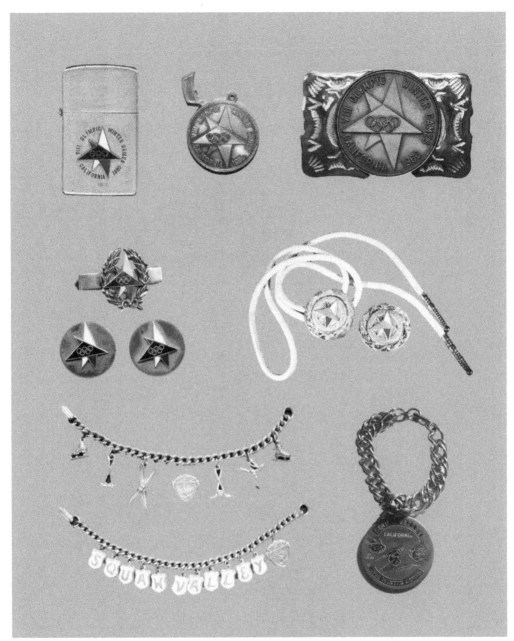

Jewelry and personal accessories adorned with symbols and logos of the Winter Olympics were popular items and reflected the culture and style of the era. Clockwise from the upper left are a stainless steel Zippo-style lighter fueled with naphtha; a perfume container locket; a silver-plated belt buckle; a bolo tie with matching pin; a bracelet with engraved fob; a ski area charm bracelet, a charm bracelet with charms denoting each of the Winter Olympics sports; clip-on earrings; and a tie bar. (Courtesy of the Batiste Family Collection.)

Visit us at
arcadiapublishing.com

Printed in the USA
CPSIA information can be obtained
at www.ICGtesting.com
LVHW070756241223
767241LV00009B/892